Freeing Verse

F.J. Keenan

BookLeaf
Publishing

Presentation by *BookLeaf Publishing*

Web: www.bookleafpub.com

E-mail: info@bookleafpub.com

ISBN: 9789357748438

First edition 2023

I have more than one muse and they will recognize their ode.

PREFACE

I took up this challenge in part to exercise my writing endurance as I encourage my students to do daily. I was also just curious to see what would come of it. To my surprise, it was revealing and truly required a lot of deep reflection. The more honest I was with this work, the better it became. If it resonates with you, reader, I hope perhaps you may find healing as I did. If anything, you know you are not the only one.

Bone-In

Buffalo wings are my culture
beginning from the hut with personal pans
and the checkered salad bar
in the small town where everyone had their party

both sets of grandparents
chortling aunts
my uncle offering to hold my birthday money
and my married parents

my sister still fights me for flats
Dad snaps them on his travels to tease me
my husband knows exactly what I want for my
birthday dinner
Yes, believe it or not, it would be my last meal

a rich and buttery acid coats my good times
so when I'm having a good day or I want one
I make a batch of wings
and I'm comforted with the past

Las Palomas

The stars in the country sky drape over like a
cool fresh sheet
the world tosses beneath it just a little slower
here.

Our great great greats transcend upon the old
fort,
the antique tractors,
and thriving tumbleweeds.

Papa sits on his porch, a ritual he believes keeps
him well,
and Nanny reads the good book and makes
copious notes.

Mountain snow runs off to the creek behind the
house and makes for a shivering wade.

We drank water from the hose,
performed tightrope acts across the cattle guard,
and shouted from the hill as loud as we could
because we could.

Our kids will take this walk,
picking up rocks

and having talks about things grown-ups are no longer brave enough to ask out loud.

Aromatherapy

On your shoulders I'd run my hands over your
head
burr length, velvet and oil.
I fingerpainted in your scent.

Sometimes really and sometimes pretend,
I slept in the back seat so you'd carry me in.
I never smelled the wrinkles now creased in
your cheek.

Your motorcycle helmet bobbled on my head.
I was never hiding in it.
I was home in your incense.

Your old white t-shirts, my favorite to sleep in,
stained and perfumed with motor oil, shop dust,
and greasy sweat.
You wouldn't wash out.

Then the lingering essence of my father
fermented.
The spoors turned cold as the whiskey stones.
It's funny what the nose can remember.

Compliments

An 18-year-old said it once when he refused to
get out of my car, because if he said I was
beautiful I would let him stay and do all else
because it didn't matter if I was younger.

A graying elder, with a chemical deception and a
loved smile said it once, because if he said I was
beautiful then age was just a number and so was
our number of related chromosomes.

A stranger said it once, in my ear on the dance
floor, because if he said I was beautiful then
taking him up on a dance meant he could take
me home too.

A father said it once, in a text while I washed the
bottle for their daughter, because if he said I was
beautiful then there was nothing wrong with a
flingy affair because it implied he cared.

"Hey beautiful"
"You're so beautiful"
"You look beautiful in that dress"
"Come on beautiful"

Now I'm messed up because I'd rather my
husband call me a good girl because beautiful is
a bad word and the subspace never hurt me.

Mistress

She arose into the air like chemical chalk dust

He helped her to her feet with an exhaled subtle kiss

I walked in on an affair I had ignored for years

She clung to him and in the air, in his eyes the most

"I'm in love with two women", he finally confessed

"You," he said honestly, "and Crystal." He inhaled her.

Get Going

8

Sometimes the footsteps
you follow are the wrong size.
Lace up those big feet.

Inner Monologue

I hugged your daughter when she cried in the
hallway today.
I cheered extra loud for your son who is stuck in
his sister's shadow.
Did someone else hug my boy while I was
away?
Does he ever wonder where or why I have to
go?

I keep my classroom stocked for the always
requested snack.
I plan with every lesson to try and go all out.
I scramble in the morning to throw breastmilk in
the backpack.
When we come home after daycare I'm ready to
pass out.

I love being a teacher and I love my students so!
I also love being a mom as I've always wanted
to be.
But there's something that I hope all my children
will know
I do my best to spread that love but there's only
one of me.

My stay-at-home mother once asked how I
would work and be a good mom.
Her question has evolved into an agonizing
psalm.

Those Who Are About To Teach

I never stress about what I will teach
I'm looking for areas someone could breach
I don't fuss over crop tops or teenage slang
I question pops or a sudden bang

I'm professionally developed on how to break
glass
After placing a tourniquet two hours can pass
I've practiced throwing textbooks across the
room
The pandemic was hard, but there was peace in
Zoom

Desks are away from the window and door
"What is this piece of rope for?"
They used to ask me this before
Now they ask "what if you can't help us
anymore?"

I don't worry about what I'll teach
They'll keep writing essays or giving a speech
My objectives will be on the board still
I just pray for the best, that this is just a drill

Artificial Intelligence

I shake my head at these times
My students talk about someone being a rizzler
Another one being a simp
They focus in 15, 30, or 60 second increments
They regurgitate the opinions on their feed
Which have evolved into their mindset

Brainwashing is a curious phenomena
Children need a screen to get through a meal
Teenagers need their ears plugged up to get
through school
Husbands join the congregation of gaming
violence and escape reality for hours on end
I succumb to the siren call of the social network
And most nights, it does answer the question
"What's for dinner?"

But when the wifi goes out or we lose power, we
scramble
We see our device dependency
How will I know the weather today if Alexa
can't tell me?
How will I remember my Grandma's birthday if
I don't save it in the calendar?

How will I know my goals if I don't write them
in my notes app?
How can I do my job without email? Without a
computer?

I'm afraid.
Battery life is determining how long we go
Before we force ourselves to cultivate a thought
of our own

Shout Out to Mrs. Buchanan

My students refused to tell me what she meant.
Did they, too, believe that girls should be fools?

Muffled giggles bubbled from a boy or two and
they all pleaded the fifth
saying "I think one of the girls should answer
this."

The girls, with guilty reluctance on their faces,
silently pleaded to move on with the reading.

Despite our setting, did they find the line stapled
on their own tongue?
Was bliss only to be found when they stilled
their rebellious intellect?

Subliminally, I whisper
"Every man was once tied to the string of a
woman whether by her body or her apron."

Victory & Hail

It's hard being the oldest
because sometimes I'm the default parent
and I don't have all the answers.

I see you glow with love's beam on your face
and I wonder if you'll get burned.

I see you carrying the team
while your "biggest fan" sleeps on the sideline.

I see you strolling through life
and I envy your ease.

I did it all first,
even if I didn't want to.

You did some things first
and I was supposed to.

When mom and dad are gone
I'll hold the earliest memories for you.

It's hard being the oldest
because maybe that means I'll die first.
How could I possibly leave you two alone?

Harry's Loss

There are some moments we try to engrave in
our memory
Looking it over finely with a magnifying glass

Burning in the moment when she looks up at
him and he says to the table
"We're getting married"
Etching in the shock, the joy, the worry

Who could forget how they felt when they knew
the baby was getting married
We hope we don't, but we might

The smolder will die down until she walks the
aisle
And then the nest will really be empty
We aren't kids anymore and never will be again

She tells me he's the one,
And in her eyes I see the ashes of the once
littlest sister
who waited in the crib for me to take her out

Comfort

On our wedding night,
we fell asleep eating cake
and chicken tenders.

Fly on the Wall

My husband's shoulders resemble the house
sparrow's egg
his cheeks are blushed, a permanent stain
hands like branches, knobbed and barked
I kiss his neck and taste the grit of salt and earth
his weary gaze shows the morning alarm and the
high 90's
Exhausted, he says, "you are so sexy"
as I don a pumping bra and flour-dusted
sweatpants
my trellis of hair tangled around my head
disheveled from the windy walk out of daycare
oil spattered glasses from the chops on the stove
2:45 written on my hand to remind me of bus
duty and a chapped kiss that tastes like
emergency chocolate
"So are you," I share a spent smile
then offer a mashed potato finger toward the
playpen

The Coronation

I braced myself
rocking
submerged
locking
When they subsided I'd surface and roar
Then I'm swept under over and over more

There is no focus
There is no control
Darkness and only my soul
I sink

I'm losing
I slip underneath the crush.

Blind. Incapacitated. Overdosed.

I feel everything.
The fiery crown

He was with me
Drowning
He was within me
Counting

Then we catch our breath

Beloved

From the moment you
arrived, I have prayed for our
immortality.

I Dreamt I Held You In My Arms

Another season, ripped from my grasp
Your daddy's sleepy smirk sneaks through his
snores
I push away and force myself to cry in silence

I wander blind beneath the covers
searching for your tiny hands
listening for your whispery breaths,
but I find the wall and hear the static of your
sound machine on the monitor

Tonight, you're in your "big boy" bed
Daddy has waited a year to have me back to
himself
But tonight, it's me who has to learn to sleep
alone

You were born in this bed. It is imprinted with
us. Our nest.
My lungs heaved over your form, feeling you
trace your knee or elbow across me
As if to say "roll over, you're hogging the bed"

I then nursed you, sometimes every hour of the
night
Checking your temperature
Watching your chest rise and fall

Then you learned to smile at me when we woke
Sometimes you would simply stare
As if to understand I was the one, your keeper

And now, I lay upon a cold salty pillow
comforting myself
training away my instincts

And Many More

Then a little mystery, a nebula of divisions
Only to emerge explosively and brilliant
Beaming your second day and onward
I reflect upon a revolution of glimmers
A star, the one which I revolve
Son, my sun, happy birthday

Encore Encore

I want to Groundhog Day us into these early
thirties
chasing him, and each other, around this little
house
these jobs, these dogs, and our hopeful garden

all our firsts

our health, apart from the occasional runny nose
ice cream on a beautiful day and laughing at the
dinner table
our parents are living and the family tree keeps
branching

let's live it again?

good morning kiss, little reaching arms, and
running late to make tea
late-night baking, mowing Grandma's yard, and
books before bedtime
exhausted, in love, and fulfilled

Happy

I'd live it again
just the same, the good and bad,
to have this life now.

Philippians

Life is full of
hard,
beautiful,
waiting,
everything,
and unknown.
But my birthday made it easy to recall the verse
I would need.